Foods That Work For You

Delectable and Gluten-Free Desserts and Drinks

Olivia M. Lake, RHN

Copyright © 2014 Olivia M. Lake

All photograph copyright © 2008 - 2014 by Olivia M. Lake. All rights reserved.

All rights reserved. No part of this book may be used, stored, reproduced or transmitted in any form or by any means, electronic, mechanical, photocopying or otherwise without prior written permission of the author and/or publisher.

ISBN 978-0-9867565-2-8 E-book 978-0-9867565-4-2

Photography: Olivia M. Lake
Food styling and recipe development/design: Olivia M. Lake
Editing/cover and design: Olivia M. Lake
Recipe testing and critiquing: Adan Schubart, Suzanne Prendergast and Olivia M. Lake

Special thanks to taste testers:
Adan Schubart
Julian Schubart – Lake
Alexandra Lake
Suzanne Prendergast
Elizabeth Rago
Graham Elliot
Quinn Myhill – Jones
Colin Schuert
Brent Eliason
Cavan Auchterlonie

Author, publisher and all other persons listed on this page cannot accept responsibility for any harm, food intoxications, infections or other bodily issues, illnesses or death and/or injuries or damages that could result from the preparation of recipes and/or consumption of these or any ingredients contained in this book.

Library and Archives Canada
Lake, Olivia Megan, 1975-
Foods That Work For You: Delectable and Gluten-Free Desserts and Drinks /
by Olivia Megan Lake
Victoria, B.C.: Olivia Megan Lake, 2014

wholeprofilehealth.dudaone.com

Other cookbooks by this author:
Foods That Work For You: Delectable and Gluten Free
ISBN 978-0-9867565-1-1 E-book 978-0-9867565-3-5

Contents:

Gluten-Free Grains / Seeds / Flours……………………………………………4

Notes……………………………………………………………………………6

Bread Goodies…………………………………………………………………7

Desserts………………………………………………………………………29

Drinks…………………………………………………………………………62

Sauces and Fillings…………………………………………………………72

Glossary………………………………………………………………………81

List of Gluten-Free Grains and Casein-Free Alternatives……………82

Index……………………………………………………………………………83

Gluten-Free Bakeries and Cafés……………………………………………87

Foods That Work For You: Delectable and Gluten-Free Desserts and Drinks

Gluten-Free Grains / Seeds / Flours

Rice

Jasmine Long-Grain   Arborio Short-Grain   Brown Rice Flakes

Red   Brown Short-Grain   Brown Long-Grain

Other Grains

Millet   Corn

Seeds

Wild or Indian Rice Brown Flax Hemp Hearts

Buckwheat Amaranth Quinoa

Grind Any Nut, Seed, or Grain, Into Flour.

Sorghum Brown Rice

Notes:

Recipes
If the ingredients, process, utensils, cook ware, temperature, elevation or operation of these recipes are altered in any way, than I cannot guarantee success.

Ways to ensure success:
- Follow instructions accurately.
- Do not let dough or batter sit unless specifically instructed to do so.
- Level off measurements.
- Electrical appliances vary so expect slight variances in cooking time and/or temperature.

Purchasing
- All ingredients for recipes can be found at organic food stores and/or your popular grocery stores.
- Purchase organic.
- Choose ingredients with the least amount of food additives and preservatives.
- Inspect fruits and vegetables and purchase only undamaged produce.
- Always check expiry date on products before purchasing.

Storage
- Always store gluten free flours in a plastic bag, inside a paper bag, in the fridge with the top properly sealed.
- Always store shelled nuts and nut flours properly sealed in the fridge or freezer.

Temperature
- For more accurate temperature conversions use the following standard formulas: $C = 5/9 (F-32)$ $F = (9/5C) + 32$. That stated, I have written in recipes, what your oven dial will most likely read.

Foods That Work For You: Delectable and Gluten-Free Desserts and Drinks

Foods That Work For You: Delectable and Gluten-Free Desserts and Drinks

Bread Goodies

Almond Cookies...................................8
Banana Bread..9
Banana Pecan Muffins...11
Blackberry Scones................................13
Buckwheat Chocolate Chip Cookies......................................14
Buckwheat Shortbread..15
Chocolate Pecan Cookies...16

Coconut Almond Cookies.................18
Corn Meal Muffins / Corn Cake......................................19
Dark Chocolate Seed Muffins...21
Ginger Molasses Cookies..23
Maple Blueberry Pretzel Tarts..................................24
Pretzel Biscuits....................................26
Snowball Shortbread.......................27

Foods That Work For You: Delectable and Gluten-Free Desserts and Drinks

Almond Cookies
Dairy Free - Chewy with a crunchy edge

Makes 8 - 3" round

Ingredients
1/2 cup light brown sugar
1 large brown egg - free run
1/4 tsp sea salt
3 tbsp 100% grapeseed oil
1/4 tsp vanilla - pure extract
1 cup ground blanched raw almonds - cold
1/2 cup sliced blanched raw almonds - frozen
1 tbsp grated lemon or orange rind (optional) - wash before grating

Other:
100% grapeseed oil or parchment paper

Method
Combine in a large mixing bowl with egg beater on medium speed: light brown sugar, egg, sea salt, grape seed oil and vanilla flavor.

Preheat oven to 350°F (180°C).

Stir in with wooden spoon: ground blanched almonds, sliced blanched almonds, lemon or orange rind (optional).
Grease or line cookie sheet with: grapeseed oil or parchment paper.

Drop, one at a time, on to parchment paper or greased cookie sheet, placed 1 - 1 1/2" apart: 1 tbsp of batter.
Place in oven on center rack.
Bake 10-12 minutes or until golden and brown around the edges.
Remove from oven.
Use metal spatula to lift cookies to cooling rack or plate.
Serve.

Tip: Do not leave warm cookies sitting on plate, as moisture will collect under the cookies and make them soggy. Place on cooling rack if not being eaten right away.

Time: Approximately 30 minutes

* **Store** in sealed container in the fridge.

# Banana Bread
Dairy Free

1 Loaf

Ingredients
1 tsp baking soda
2/3 cup stone ground sorghum flour
2 cups organic brown rice flour
1/4 tsp sea salt
4 large brown eggs
1/2 tsp vanilla - pure extract
8 tbsp 100% grapeseed oil
1 1/2 cups packed ripe banana - 3 bananas peeled and chopped or mashed
1/4 cup cow's milk or nut milk
3/4 cup light brown sugar - lightly packed
1/2 cup broken up raw pecans
3 tbsp hot tap water

Other
Parchment paper

Method
Mix in large bowl, with wooden spoon: baking soda, sorghum flour, brown rice flour and sea salt.
Combine in: brown eggs, vanilla flavor, grapeseed oil, bananas and milk.

Preheat oven to 350°F (180°C).

Combine in remaining ingredients.
Line inside of 9" x 5" x 3" loaf pan with: parchment paper - press firmly into corners and seams and trim to 1/2" overhang.
Pour batter into pan. Scrape out bowl and level with rubber spatula.
Place in oven, on centre rack.
Bake for 55-60 minutes, or until color of bread is brown and when poked with knife, knife comes out clean.
Remove from oven and let cool slightly.
Grab edges of paper and lift to cooling rack or to a bread board.
Slice.
Serve warm topped with unsalted butter (optional).
Place loaf on cooling rack.

Time: 1 hr. 15 min.

- **Store** in sealed container or wrap loaf in parchment paper and place in a closed plastic bag in the fridge or freezer.

- **Reheat** on oven-safe dish in toaster oven or stove oven, at 200°F (100°C) for approximately 3 minutes.

Banana Pecan Muffins
Dairy Free

Makes 8

Ingredients
1 cup brown rice flour
1/3 cup sorghum flour
1/8 tsp sea salt
4 large brown eggs
2 tsp baking powder - magic
6 tbsp grapeseed oil
1/4 cup natural brown sugar - Demerara
1/4 tsp vanilla - pure extract
1 regular sized very ripe banana - skin removed or 1/2 cup fresh mango and nectarine - cubed
1/3 cup broken up pecans or walnuts
Topping
Peanut Taffy Topping - optional crumble top (pg.78)

Other
Large baking cups

Method
Prepare Peanut Taffy Topping, stove top method. Cook 15 minutes before turning down. After removing from burner keep whisking until mixture starts to set and ball. Add and stir in: 1 tbsp and 1 tsp sweetened shredded coconut and 1/2 - 3/4 cup almond flour. Place in fridge.

Preheat oven to 350°F (180°C).

Blend in large bowl, with electric beater on low speed, until well combined: all ingredients - exclude walnuts, pecans, and Peanut Taffy Topping crumble.
Combine in with wooden spoon or fork: pecans or walnuts.
Line muffin forms with baking cups.
Scoop batter out and fill baking cups.
Top each muffin with approximately 1tbsp of: Peanut Taffy Topping crumble.
Place in lower 1/3 of oven or 6" up from bottom.
Bake 18-23 minutes. Muffins should be browned and chopstick comes out clean when muffin is poked through its center, or top feels set when touched.
Remove from oven and let cool on wire rack until you are able to handle. Move muffins to cooling rack.
Serve warm or cold.
Slice and top with butter (optional).

Time: 45-50 minutes (includes clean up. Does not include cooling time or Topping time)

- **Store** in a sealed container or in a properly sealed plastic bag in the fridge or freezer.

- **Reheat** at 200 °F or on toast.

Blackberry Scones
Dairy Free

Makes 7 - Large

Ingredients
2 medium brown eggs
6 tbsp 100% grapeseed oil
3 cups organic brown rice flower
1/4 tsp sea salt
4 1/2 tsp baking powder - magic
3 tbsp pure organic maple syrup
1 cup almond milk - unsweetened/original
1 1/2 cups fresh blackberries

Other
Unsalted butter to grease sheet, or parchment paper

Method
Preheat oven to 350°F (180°C).

Beat with egg beater until yolk is completely broken: eggs and oil.
Grease or line metal baking or cookie sheet with: butter or parchment paper.
Mix in with wooden spoon: remaining ingredients.
Combine dough until thick and sticky.
Divide dough into 7 equal pieces (1/2 cup each) by scooping dough into the measuring cup and giggling it upside down until dough plops out into your hand. Toss dough back and forth between cupped palms until ball is formed.

Tip: Wash and dry hands when half way through dough. Then continue forming balls.

Place on baking sheet, then place in oven.
Set timer for 20 minutes.
Bake until dry on top, and cooked all the way through.
Serve warm with unsalted butter or coconut butter.

Serve As a Dessert
Warm thoroughly.
Gently slice in half.
Fill with: berry sauce.
Top with: berry sauce and whip cream (optional).

Time: 35-40 minutes

- **Store**, when completely cooled, in a sealed container in the fridge.

- **Reheat,** all the way through, in convection toaster oven or regular oven, before serving. Around 250°F (120°C) on warm setting, or toast.

Buckwheat Chocolate Chip Cookies
A chocolate chip cookie with a light poppy seed flavor

Makes 12

Ingredients
2 large brown eggs - free run
1/4 tsp vanilla - pure extract
1/4 tsp sea salt
3/4 cup brown sugar
1 cup organic brown rice flour
1/3 cup buckwheat flour
1/4 cup hot tap water
1/2 cup melted (warm) unsalted butter
1/2 cup chocolate chips - dark

Other
Unsalted butter

Method
Preheat oven to 350°F (180°C).

Whisk in large bowl: eggs, vanilla, sea salt, and brown sugar.
Stir in with wooden spoon: brown rice flour and buck wheat flour.
Combine in: water.
Melt in small copper/stainless pot over medium heat or in microwave oven then combine in: 1/2 cup butter.
Grease flat cookie sheet with a thin layer of: butter.
Stir in: chocolate chips.

Place on to greased cookie sheet: 1 heaping tbsp of cookie dough for each cookie.
Cook 10-12 minutes or until golden brown around edges.
Cool on pan 3 minutes, remove with metal spatula.
Place on cooling rack or serve.

Time: Approximately 30 minutes

* **Store** in sealed container in the fridge.

Buckwheat Shortbread
Makes 16

Ingredients
1/2 - 3/8 cup unsalted butter - melted
4 tbsp icing sugar
1 tsp white sugar
1/8 tsp sea salt
1 cup buckwheat flour
1 tsp vanilla - pure extract
1 large brown egg
Topping
Premium cocoa
Icing sugar

Method
Preheat oven to 350°F (180°C).

Note: For a more, crunchy cookie use: 1/2 cup butter.

For a softer cookie use: 3/8 cup butter.

Melt over low to medium heat: butter.
Combine in mixing bowl: all ingredients.
Use a tablespoon to shape cookies before placing on the cookie sheet.
Place in oven, on center rack.
Bake 15 minutes.
Rotate pan half way through baking.
Sprinkle with: Topping.
Remove from sheet with metal spatula.

Time: 35-40 minutes

* **Store** in sealed container or wax lined tin or container in fridge or freezer.

Chocolate Pecan Cookies
Dairy Free - Soft and wonderfully textured

Makes 12

Ingredients
1/2 tsp baking soda
1/3 cup stone ground sorghum flour
1 cup organic brown rice flour
1/8 tsp sea salt
2 large brown eggs
1/4 tsp vanilla flavor
3 tbsp 100% grapeseed oil
1/2 cup light brown sugar - lightly packed or for a more spongy/softer cookie - 1/3 cup organic agave nectar - amber
1/4 cup broken up raw pecans
1/2 cup dark chocolate chips
2 tbsp almond milk - original/unsweetened

Other
Parchment paper or unsalted butter

Method
Have all ingredients cold.
Mix in large bowl with wooden spoon: baking soda, sorghum flour, rice flour and sea salt.
Combine in: eggs, vanilla and oil.

Preheat oven to 350°F (180°C)

Combine in: sugar or nectar, pecans, chocolate chips and almond milk.

Grease or line cookie sheet with: unsalted butter or parchment paper - trim paper to size of sheet.
Place on cookie sheet approximately 1" apart: 1 heaping tbsp of batter per cookie.
Place in oven, on center rack. Bake 10-12 minutes. Rotate cookie sheet half way through cooking time.
Remove from oven. Use a metal spatula to place cookies on serving plate or cooling rack.
Serve warm or cold.

Time: Approximately 30 minutes

- **Store** in sealed container, tin or plastic bag lined with parchment paper in the fridge or freezer.

- **Reheat** on plate, in toaster oven or stove oven, at 200°F (100°C) for approximately 3 minutes.

Coconut Almond Cookies

Dairy Free - Chewy and soft

Makes 6 - 4" round or 9 - 2 1/2" round

Ingredients
1 cup light brown sugar
2 large brown eggs - free run
1/2 tsp sea salt
6 tbsp 100% grapeseed oil
1/2 tsp vanilla - pure extract
2 cups ground blanched almonds - cold
1/2 cup sliced blanched raw almonds - frozen
1/2 cup shredded coconut
1 tbsp finely grated lemon rind (optional) - rind from 1 organic lemon (wash well before grating)

Other
Parchment paper or butter

Method
Mix thoroughly in large mixing bowl with egg beater on medium speed: sugar, eggs, sea salt, oil, and vanilla.

Preheat oven to 350°F (180°C)

Stir in with wooden spoon: almonds, coconut and lemon rind (optional).
Grease or line cookie sheet with: unsalted butter or parchment paper - trim paper to size of sheet.
Drop on to cookie sheet, placed 1" apart: 2 1/2 tbsp of batter per cookie.
Place cookies in oven on center rack.
Bake 14-16 minutes, or until golden brown around edges. Rotate cookie sheet half way through baking.
Remove from oven and use metal spatula to lift cookies from parchment paper.
Serve.
Cool on wire rack before storing.

Tip: Do not leave warm cookies sitting on plate, this will make them soggy.

Time: Approximately 35 minutes

* **Store** in sealed container in the fridge or freezer.

Cornmeal Muffins / Corn Cake
Dairy Free - Still moist the next day, and the next

Makes 12

Ingredients
1 cup brown rice flour
1/3 cup sorghum flour
1/3 cup corn meal
1/3 cup brown natural sugar
1/4 tsp sea salt
2 tsp baking powder - magic
1/2 tsp baking soda
1/4 tsp vanilla - pure extract (omit for dinner cornmeal muffins)
3 large brown eggs
3 tbsp grapeseed oil
1 3/4 cups almond milk - original/unsweetened, breeze brand - substitute the 3/4 cup with freshly squeezed orange juice (2 large oranges) for corn cake

Other
Giant paper liners or cups
Parchment paper for cake
8" round pan for cake

Method
Preheat oven to 350°F (180°C)

Wisk dry ingredients together in mixing bowl. Make hole in dry mix.
Add: eggs, oil, and almond milk.
Combine. Batter should be thick and soupy.
Place liners in ceramic muffin forms or line pan for cake.
Fill each liner with: 1/3 cup of batter for muffins. Leave approximately 1/4" from batter to top of liner; or fill cake pan.
Place in lower 1/3 of oven.
Cook 20-25 minutes / cake 35 minutes or until center does not jiggle and is golden in color.
Remove from oven and move to cooling rack / cake - peel paper away from edges.
Serve warm with butter and/or honey; or prepare as a dessert and coat with: Cream Cheese Icing (pg. 75). Serve with whip cream, berry sauce and/or your favorite citrus liqueur.

Time: 35-40 minutes / 60-70 minutes

* **Store** left over batter in fridge in glass or ceramic container with lid. Store muffins or cake in sealed bag or container. Batter good for 1-2 days.

Dark Chocolate Seed Muffins
Dairy Free

Makes 9

Ingredients
1 tsp baking soda
2/3 cup stone ground sorghum flour
2 cups organic brown rice flour
1/4 tsp sea salt
4 large brown eggs
1/2 tsp vanilla - pure extract
6 tbsp 100% grapeseed oil
1 1/2 packed cups ripe banana - 3 bananas peeled and chopped or mashed
3/4 cup light brown sugar - lightly packed
1/2 cup pure dark chocolate chips
1/2 cup raw unsalted sunflower seeds
2 tbsp hot water

Other
Large baking cups
100% grapeseed oil
Plastic food bags or zip lock bags

Method
Mix in large mixing bowl, with wooden spoon: baking soda, sorghum flour, rice flour and sea salt.
Combine in with wooden spoon: eggs, vanilla flavor, grapeseed oil and bananas.

Preheat oven to 350°F (180°C).

Combine in: brown sugar, chocolate chips, sunflower seeds and hot water.
Grease just the tops or surrounding edges of muffin forms with: 100% grape seed oil.
Line the inside of the muffin forms with: large baking cups.
Scoop batter into cups.
Place in oven, on centre rack.
Bake for 30-35 minutes.
Remove from oven when color of muffins is brown and when poked with knife, knife comes out clean.
Let muffins cool slightly.
Slice and serve warm topped with unsalted butter (optional).
Place muffins on cooling rack.

Time: 50 minutes

- **Store** in sealed container or place in a closed plastic bag. Place in fridge or freezer.

- **Reheat** on oven safe dish, in toaster oven or stove oven, at 200°F (100°C) for approximately 3 minutes, or serve cold.

Ginger Molasses Cookies

Dairy Free - A soft cookie with a chewy crispy edge

10 large or 12 small

Ingredients
1/8 tsp sea salt
1/2 cup white sugar
1/8 cup organic unsulphured molasses - scrape out measure with rubber spatula
1/2 tsp vanilla - pure extract
1 large brown egg
1 tsp ginger
2 tbsp 100% grapeseed oil
1/3 cup plus 1/8 cup ground blanched almonds or almond powder
1/2 cup plus 1/8 cup stone ground sorghum flour
1/4 cup organic brown rice flour
1/8 cup hot water (only if necessary)

Other
Parchment paper or unsalted butter

Method
Combine with egg beater in large mixing bowl: sea salt, white sugar, molasses, vanilla, egg, ginger and grapeseed oil.

Preheat oven to 350°F (180°C).

Combine in with wooden spoon: ground blanched almonds or almond powder, sorghum flour and brown rice flour.

Batter should be moist and thick. If it seems too dry add: 1/8 cup hot water.
Grease cookie sheet with a thin layer of: unsalted butter or parchment paper - trim to size.
Place on cookie sheet: 1 heaping tbsp of dough per cookie.
Place in oven and set timer for 10 minutes.
Remove from oven when done. Use a metal spatula to remove cookies from sheet and place on cooling rack.

Tip: These cookies are soft and chewy around the edges, scraping any stuck on cookie off the edge of the metal spatula between cookies will prevent the cookies from breaking as you remove them from the sheet.

Serve cold.

Time: 45 minutes

 ❋ **Store** in fridge in sealed container.

Maple Blueberry Pretzel Tarts
Dairy Free - **Makes 12**

Ingredients
2 tbsp pure maple syrup
5 tbsp grapeseed oil
2 large brown eggs - separated (keep whites aside in separate bowl)
2 tsp baking powder - magic
1/4 tsp sea salt
1/4 tsp vanilla - pure extract
1 1/4 cups plus 1 tbsp brown rice flour
2 tsp hot water
Topping
1 tbsp grapeseed oil
1/3 cup or approximately 120 frozen wild woodland blueberries
2-3 tbsp maple syrup
Approximately 1 tsp black lava salt

Other
Parchment paper

Method
Combine thoroughly with wooden spoon, in large mixing bowl: all Ingredients - excluding egg whites.
Blend with egg beater until white and soft peaks form then add to other ingredients in large mixing bowl and combine in: 2 egg whites.
Line flat cookie sheet with: parchment paper - cut to size and place over sheet.

Preheat oven to 375°F (205°C).

Rub a little oil on palms.
Knead dough several times, until well formed.
Scoop and place on hand: approximately 1 tbsp of dough. Roll into a well formed ball between palms. Place on clean, dry surface area and roll, with palms, into a 7" long strip approximately 3/4" round. Gently turn ends up to make circle then lift down into center, across one another to form an "x" overtop of horizontal piece to form pretzel shape. See image.
Move to lined cookie sheet.
Brush onto tops and around base of pretzel tarts: oil (1 tbsp is enough for all).
Remove from freezer and gently press into dough in each pretzel hole: 3-5 blueberries.
Drizzle each, pretzel tart with: maple syrup.
Bake 22 minutes.
Remove from oven and lift to cooling rack.
Sprinkle with: black lava salt.

Serve cold.

Time: 1hr. 10 min. (includes cleanup)

* **Store** in sealed glass container. Lasts longer in fridge or freezer.

Pretzel Biscuits
Dairy Free

Makes 12

Ingredients
2 tbsp pure maple syrup
5 tbsp grapeseed oil
2 large brown eggs - separated (keep whites aside in separate bowl)
2 tsp baking powder - magic
1/4 tsp sea salt
1/4 tsp vanilla - pure extract
1 cup plus 1 tbsp white rice flour
1/4 cup sorghum flour
2 tsp hot water
Topping
1-2 tsp black lava salt
1 tbsp grapeseed oil

Other
Wax paper
Flat cookie sheet

Method
Follow instructions for the Maple Blueberry Pretzel Tarts, omitting: blueberries and maple syrup topping.
Press on to each biscuit, to coat evenly: black lava salt.
Brush on, using a gentle dabbing motion: grapeseed oil.

Bake 22 minutes.

Remove from oven and lift to cooling rack.

Serve cold.

Time: 1 hour

Snowball Shortbread
A soft light cookie

Makes 10 balls

Ingredients
1/2 cup unsalted butter - melted
1/8 cup icing sugar
1 tsp white sugar
1/8 tsp sea salt
1 cup brown rice flour
Topping
Premium cocoa
Icing sugar

Method
Preheat oven to 350°F (180°C).

Melt butter in small pot over low to medium heat.
Combine in mixing bowl: all ingredients.
Shape cookies before placing on the cookie sheet.
Place in oven, on center rack.
Bake 20 minutes.
Rotate pan half way through baking.
Sprinkle cookies with: Topping.
Serve when completely cooled.
Remove from sheet with metal spatula.

Note: Best served the following day.

Time: 35-40 minutes

* **Store** in sealed container or wax lined tin in fridge or freezer.

Foods That Work For You: Delectable and Gluten-Free Desserts and Drinks

Desserts

Amber Corn..30	Lemon Almond Torte..48
Apple Tarts..32	Mango Custard...............................49
Banana Coconut Cream Pie...33	Nutty Vanilla Lemon Meringue............50
Banana Custard....................................35	Peach Logan Custard.......................52
Boule De Neige À La Mousse..36	Pie Crust.......................................54
Brownie Cake.......................................38	Pie Crust.......................................55
Cocoa Rice Puff Refrigerator Cookies..40	Pie Crust – White..............................56
Cocoa Torte...41	Pumpkin Custard............................57
Coffee Toffee Bars................................43	Raw Fruit Pudding..........................58
Dark Chocolate Cake............................45	Sunflower Chocolates......................59
Layered Raspberry Squares...............46	Whole Egg Macaroon Base/ Cookies...61

Amber Corn

This corn is sweet and buttery, and sure to delight your taste buds

Makes 8 cups

Ingredients
1/8 cup vegetable oil
1/3 cup popcorn
1/2 cup mixture of shelled raw almonds, pecans and walnuts

Amber sauce:
1/2 cup salted butter
2 cups powdered light brown sugar
1/3 cup organic raw blue agave nectar - amber

Other:
Parchment paper

Method
Coat the bottom of a large 16 cup, or 4 liter, copper/stainless pot with: vegetable oil.
Turn burner onto maximum.
Place pot with oil and popcorn in it on burner, with lid on.
Lift pot off burner by handles, frequently, and shake. Once popcorn is popping turn off burner, leave pot on burner for a few seconds, than lift an inch or two above burner and shake, then hold steady above burner. Continue this motion until all the popcorn has popped.
Remove lid and set aside while preparing the amber sauce.

Melt over medium heat in a 4 cup, or 1litre, heavy sauce pan, with lid on: salted butter.
Add to butter (when completely melted), and stir in with wooden spoon until thick: brown sugar and agave nectar.
Turn burner up to high.
Stir frequently until boiling, approximately 8 minutes. Turn off heat, leave pot on burner and keep stirring until sugar sauce has cooled to simmering. Leave on burner let sit for 7 minutes, remove from burner and stir.
Add (in large pot) to popcorn: almonds, pecans and walnuts
Scrape and pour amber sauce over popcorn mixture. Use a spoon or rubber spatula to gently and thoroughly fold in amber sauce.

Preheat toaster oven to 300°F (150°C).

Place a thin layer of popcorn mixture on baking sheet or pan.
Bake 4 minutes then remove.
Flip pieces and separate any clumps.
Place back in oven for 6 minutes.
Remove and let cool, approximately 5 minutes.
Break apart and serve when completely cool.

Time: 50 min. - 1 hr.

- Store in sealed container in a cool, dry and dark cupboard, or in a closed tin lined with parchment paper on counter, away from heat and moisture.

Apple Tarts
Dairy Free

Makes 8

Ingredients
Crust
1/8 tsp sea salt
1 cup brown rice flour
2 tbsp corn starch
1/2 cup sorghum flour
1 tbsp fine white granulated sugar
5 tbsp grapeseed oil
1 large brown egg
2 tbsp hot water
1/4 tsp cinnamon
1/4 tsp vanilla - pure extract
Filling
1 tbsp corn starch
1/4 tsp cinnamon
Pinch of nutmeg
2 sliced Gala apples
1/2 cup water
Toppings
Brown sugar and Cinnamon or
Peanut Taffy Topping (pg.78)

Other
Ceramic muffin form
Corn starch

Method
Cook in small pot over medium heat, with lid on, until apples are soft: filling.
Stir and mash with fork.
Place rack in lower third of oven.

Preheat oven to 350°F (180°C).

Combine in mixing bowl: all crust ingredients.
Take small portions of the dough to form, approximately 1/4" thick shells in the muffin forms, by pressing into bottom and up sides of form. Reserve a handful for tops.
Cook 5 minutes.
Fill with: prepared filling.
Use a little corn starch to flour area for rolling dough.
Roll out the handful of dough until 1/8" thick, slice and place slices in criss-cross pattern over top of tart.
Place back in oven for 10 minutes.
Remove from oven and sprinkle tops with brown sugar and cinnamon, or drizzle Peanut Taffy Topping and sprinkle with cinnamon.
Place back in oven for 5 minutes.

Time: 1 hour

* **Store** in sealed container in fridge or freezer.

Banana Coconut Cream Pie
Dairy Free

Makes 8 generous sized servings

Ingredients
Crust
1 large brown egg - free run
1/4 tsp vanilla - pure extract
1/8 tsp sea salt
1/4 cup white sugar
4 tbsp 100% grapeseed oil
1 1/4 cups organic brown rice flour
Filling
1 3/4 cups of organic coconut milk - 1 - 144ml can - unsweetened
1 1/2 cups banana - 4 medium ripe, broken up and packed
1/3 cup organic brown rice flower
1 tsp organic vanilla flavor
1 large brown egg - free run
Toppings
Banana
Whip cream

Other
9" x 2" glass pie plate

Method
Preheat toaster oven to 325°F (165 °C).

Add to large mixing bowl and blend with eggbeater until well combined and pale yellow: all crust ingredients - except oil and flour.

Add and stir in with wooden spoon until all flour has absorbed liquids and forms into dough: grape seed oil and brown rice flour.
Collect excess dough off bottom of bowl and sides of spoon and place on top of dough. Knead dough in bowl a few times, form into a ball and then pick up and flatten between palms. Place in centre of: 9" x 2" glass pie dish.
Press (with fingers closed) from centre out, pushing dough out and up sides of dish. Use this pushing down and forward motion to form an even layer of dough.

Tip: Keep hands clean and dry to prevent dough from sticking to hands.

Place pie shell in center of oven and set timer for 10 minutes.
Prepare Filling.
Pour into large mixing bowl and stir with fork: organic unsweetened coconut milk.
Peel, break apart, add to coconut milk and mash with fork or blend in: 4 medium ripe bananas.
Add and mix thoroughly with wooden spoon: brown rice flower, organic vanilla and egg.

Pour filling into crust, using spatula to scrape sides of bowl and to level out the filling.
Place in toaster oven and turn up to 350°F (180°C).
Bake for 40 minutes.
Remove from oven. Knife should come out a little wet and pie should jiggle a little.
Let pie cool. Place in fridge to cool completely before serving.
Serve on its own or with whip cream and sliced bananas.

Time: 1hr. 25 min.

- **Store** in fridge in sealed container or cover pie plate. Freeze in sealed container.

Banana Custard
Dairy Free / Vegan / Raw

2 - 1/2 cup servings

Ingredients
1/2 tsp vanilla - pure extract
1 cup - 2 smaller peeled bananas broken up
2 tsp lemon juice (freshly squeezed)
1/2 cup coconut milk solids from top of can
Less than 1/8 tsp sea salt - very small pinch
2 tbsp almond milk - original/unsweetened, breeze brand
Topping
1/4 tsp freshly squeezed lemon juice
1 tbsp golden brown sugar
1 tsp coconut milk

Method
Wash all fruit and dry.
Blend on high in large mixing bowl or blender, until smooth and combined: all ingredients - except Topping.
Divide evenly into custard cups and place in fridge.

Prepare Topping. Mix in small bowl until well combined: Topping ingredients.
Spread gently and evenly over top of custard and place back in fridge to chill 30 minutes minimum.

Time: 1 hour

Boule De Neige À La Mousse
Makes 40 - 46 balls

Ingredients
.472kg block of dark couverture chocolate
(l x w x d) 4 3/4" x 3 1/4" x 1 1/2"
1/4 cup cream 10% M.F.
1/4 cup organic coconut milk solids
1/2 cup ground blanched almonds

Other
Parchment paper

Method
Measure up block 2 1/2" and make a mark with a knife. Place block up right in a small copper/stainless pot and melt over very low to minimum heat. Hold top of block moving it continuously, until melted to your line. When melted chocolate level reaches line, continue to melt bar another 4 minutes. Remove pot from heat.
Remove bar from pot and place dry side down on bread board or plate.
Stir in with rubber spatula, until combined: cream and coconut milk solids from top of can.
Scrape off as much of the chocolate on the inside walls of the pot as you can before placing in fridge to cool. Stir occasionally with metal spoon. Cool until wet and thick like batter, approximately 18 minutes.
Remove from fridge and give one more stir with spoon, then drop:

4 - 1/2 level tbsp of chocolate mixture into 1/2 cup ground blanched almonds.

Tip: Use a small spoon, using a circular motion, to scoop chocolate out of measuring spoon.

Roll chocolate around until covered in the ground blanched almonds, pick up and roll between palms to form a ball, place on waxed paper, or layer chocolates between waxed paper layers in a sealed tin or other sealed container.

Tip: Wipe excess almond grounds off your hands before scooping more chocolate from the pot. This will ensure a smooth texture to the center of the chocolates.

Serve right away.

Time: 1hr. 40min.

- **Store** in a sealed container in the refrigerator or freezer and remove chocolates as needed. Best if left to thaw before serving. When transporting, keep cool.

Brownie Cake

A soft, moist, rich cake sweetened with fruit

Makes 8 large slices - Cake is 9" round by 1 1/4" deep

Ingredients
3 frozen peach slices - unsweetened
2 banana chunks - broken off peeled banana
Coconut pineapple juice - no preservatives or artificial flavors
1/2 cup salted butter
1/2 tsp vanilla - pure extract
2 large eggs
1 cup organic apple juice
1/2 cup pineapple coconut juice - no preservatives or artificial flavors
1/2 cup premium cocoa
1 1/2 cups organic brown rice flour
1/8 tsp baking soda
1/4 tsp baking powder - magic
3/4 cup pure dark chocolate chips
Toppings
Unsalted butter
Ice cream
Whip cream
Raspberry Sauce (pg.79)

Method
Place in blender, blend on high for 1 minute then set aside: peach slices, banana, and coconut pineapple juice - this should total 1/2 cup.

Place rack in center of oven.

Grease 10" round glass pie dish and set aside, use: unsalted butter.
Place over medium heat in small copper/stainless pot swirling occasionally: 1/2 cup salted butter.
Whisk together thoroughly in large mixing bowl: vanilla flavor, eggs, apple juice, and pineapple coconut juice.
Combine in with spoon when butter is almost melted: cocoa.
Remove from heat when simmering.
Combine into egg mixture with wooden spoon: brown rice flour, baking soda and baking powder.
Combine in: cocoa/butter and 1/2 cup blended fruit and juice. Scrape pot out with rubber spatula.

Preheat oven to 350°F (180°C).

Note: If you are cooking in a new toaster oven with ceramic elements preheat to 300°F (150°C).

Melt in small copper/stainless pot over low heat, stirring frequently: chocolate chips.
Combine melted chocolate into batter.
Pour batter into greased glass pie dish. Use rubber spatula to scrape out bowl.

Place in oven and cook for 20 minutes. There will be cracks on top of cake.
Prepare Toppings: organic whipping cream and berry sauce - these are optional.
Serve warm with ice cream or organic whipping cream and Raspberry Sauce from this book.

Time: 60 minutes

- **Store** in closed container and place in fridge or freezer.

- **Reheat** in toaster oven at 250°F (120°C) on oven proof plate or dish for approximately 8 minutes.

Cocoa Rice Puff Refrigerator Cookies

Dairy Free / Vegan

Makes 36 - 38

Ingredients
1 cup organic coconut milk
1/2 cup cocoa powder
1 tsp vanilla - pure extract
1/2 cup organic agave nectar - amber
2 cups of oat flakes
1/8 tsp sea salt
1/2 cup raw hulled sunflower seeds
1 tbsp sesame seeds
2 cups organic rice puff cereal
1/2 cup coconut - shredded

Method
Whisk in mixing bowl: coconut milk, cocoa powder, vanilla flavor and agave nectar.
Combine in with wooden spoon: oat flakes, sea salt, sunflower seeds, sesame seeds, organic rice puff cereal and shredded coconut.
Roll into balls and/or form into squares: approximately 1 tbsp each.
Place onto ceramic or glass dish and place in fridge for about 20-30 minutes.

Note: You may use a metal dish or pan but line it with wax paper to prevent metallic taste from being absorbed.

When they are dry to touch, they are ready to serve.
Serve a few in a dish topped with organic whip cream (optional).

Time: 50-60 minutes

- **Store** in fridge or in a sealed container or zip lock bags when freezing.

Cocoa Torte

Dairy free - A delicious moist torte with a citrus twist

Serves 8

Ingredients
3 tbsp 100% grapeseed oil
1/2 cup light brown sugar
6 large brown egg yolks and whites
1 cup lightly packed powdered almonds
1/4 tsp vanilla flavor
Approximately 1 1/2 tbsp - 2 tbsp juice of 1/2 a medium lemon - seeds removed
Grated zest of 1/2 a medium lemon
3 tbsp premium cocoa (dairy free)

Other
8" x 2" round pan

Method
Line pan with: parchment paper - trim off excess. Leave just enough overhang to grab onto with fingertips, and then set aside.
Beat in a large bowl with egg beater on low to medium speed until thick and pale yellow: grapeseed oil, brown sugar and egg yolks.
Rinse eggbeaters off when finished and dry completely.

Preheat toaster oven to 325 °F (165 °C).

Stir in with wooden spoon: powdered almonds, vanilla flavor, lemon juice, lemon zest, and cocoa.
Beat in another medium or large bowl, on medium speed until white and just starting to form peaks: egg whites.
Pour egg whites into almond mixture and fold in until combined.
Scrape batter into the lined tin and spread evenly.
Place in centre of toaster oven.
Bake for 25-35 minutes or until browned on top and toothpick comes out mostly clean but torte is moist.
Let cool in pan for 1/2 an hour then grab edges of wax paper and lift torte out carefully and set on counter or breadboard to cool completely.
Serve with organic whip cream and/or your favorite berry sauce or liqueur. A light coffee or latte, complement this dish.

Time: 1 hr. 20 min.

* **Store** wrapped in parchment paper, in sealed container in fridge or freezer.

Coffee Toffee Bars
25 bars

Ingredients
Base
4 tbsp decaf bold espresso roast
1 1/2 cups filtered water
1 cup blanched slivered raw almonds- granulated (you may buy pre-ground blanched raw almonds, however the consistency will be very different)
1/4 cup 1 % milk
1 cup organic brown rice flower
1/2 cup light brown sugar
1 large brown egg
1 3/4 cups shredded coconut - unsweetened
.472kg block of dark couverture chocolate- (l x w x d) 4 3/4" x 3 1/4" x 1 1/2"

Filling
3 cups light brown sugar
1/2 tsp sea salt
1 cup unsalted butter
4 large brown eggs
1 cup stone ground sorghum flour

Topping
Couverture chocolate
1/2 cup organic 10% M.F. cream

Other
9 1/2" x 9 1/2" x 2" ceramic casserole dish

Method
Prepare Base. Brew In coffee machine: espresso roast and water.
Blend in blender, on high until granulated: blanched slivered raw almonds.
Measure out, add to small copper/stainless pot and warm over medium heat until steaming, then pour into large mixing bowl: 3/4 cup coffee and the milk.

Preheat oven to 350°F (180°C).

Combine in with wooden spoon or electric beater on low: brown rice flower, ground almonds, sugar, egg and coconut.
Measure 1 1/2" up chocolate block and draw a line across. Block should be 3 1/4" across and 1 1/2" thick.
Place upright in small copper/stainless saucepan over minimum heat and keep upright while melting down to your line.
Swirl block occasionally to melt evenly.
Use a rubber spatula to scrape chocolate into batter in large mixing bowl.
Combine thoroughly.
Spread with fingers, a thin layer over base and walls of a casserole dish: of butter.
Pour batter into casserole dish and spread evenly.
Place in oven and set timer for 35 minutes.

Remove from oven. Top will be dry to touch. Turn oven off and set cooked base aside to cool.
Prepare Filling. Mix in small copper/stainless pot over low heat with wooden spoon until butter is dissolved and filling ingredients are well combined: sugar, sea salt and butter.
Remove from heat.
Separate: eggs (yolk from white).
Place yolks in pot with sugar and butter, put back over heat whisking until thick and brown color lightens. Remove from heat and set aside on cool surface, whisk 3 more minutes. Use a rubber spatula to scrape center filling into another bowl or pot and place in fridge. Stir occasionally to speed cooling. When lukewarm remove from fridge and stir in thoroughly: sorghum flour.
Pour filling over base and level with rubber spatula.

Prepare Topping. Melt chocolate. Follow previous instructions for this process. When all chocolate has melted combine in: cream.
Pour over toffee centre and use rubber spatula to scrape pot and spread evenly.
Place dish in fridge to harden chocolate.
Cut into 5 even rows. Cut again perpendicular to those rows to create squares.
Serve.

Time: 3.5 hours

- **Store** only what you will eat in a week in the fridge in a closed container. Put the rest in the freezer in a sealed container. Thaw at room temperature, on serving plate or in open container, for 10 minutes.

Dark Chocolate Cake

A solid, very rich chocolate cake with a coffee like after taste

Serves 12 - 14

Ingredients
1/2 cup apple juice
A few small chunks of banana
1/2 cup salted butter - melted
1/2 tsp vanilla - pure extract
2 large brown eggs
1 cup apple juice - from concentrate
1/2 cup coconut milk solids from top of can
1 1/4 cups premium cocoa
1 1/2 cups white rice flour
1 tsp baking powder - magic
1/4 cup golden brown sugar
1/3 cup plus 1/8 cup raspberry lemonade

Toppings
Raspberry sauce
Sliced cherries
Dark Chocolate Icing (pg.76)
Whip cream

Other
Parchment paper
2" x 8" round cake pan

Method
Melt over low heat, stirring frequently: butter and flour.
Add to large mixing bowl: all other ingredients.

Preheat oven to 350°F (180°C).

Blend in until all ingredients are well combined: butter and flour.
Line 1 3/4" deep x 7 3/4" round cake pan with: parchment paper - gently press and form into place.
Pour cake mix into lined cake pan.
Cook 60 minutes, or until knife comes out of center clean.
Cool cake in pan 45 minutes - 1 hour, then lift to cooling rack and gently peel wax paper away from sides. Let cake cool another 15 minutes before completely removing wax paper.
Cut cake in half, when completely cool.
Prepare Dark Chocolate Icing and other favorite toppings or center fillings.
Apply icing and filling to center, place top back on and finish icing the outside of the cake.
Slice.
Serve.

Time: 1hr. 30 min. (see individual topping recipes for more times)

* **Store** in sealed container in fridge or freezer.

Layered Raspberry Squares
Makes 16 squares

Ingredients
2 large brown eggs
1/2 tsp vanilla - pure extract
1 tsp baking soda
6 tbsp 100% grapeseed oil
1/4 tsp sea salt
1/2 cup brown sugar - golden
1/4 cup almond flour
2 cups organic brown rice flour
Sauce
2 cups frozen unsweetened raspberries
1/3 cup finely granulated white sugar
Topping
3/4 cup raw sliced almonds

Other
Unsalted butter
9 1/2" x 9 1/2" x 2" ceramic baking dish

Method
Prepare Raspberry Sauce (pg.79)
Combine well, in large mixing bowl, with egg beater: all ingredients - except: flour, sauce, topping and butter.
Add and mix in with wooden spoon: flour.

Preheat oven to 325°F (165°C).

Grease base and sides of ceramic baking dish with: unsalted butter.
Use buttered fingers to separate dough into two even parts. Place one half in base of dish and spread using a pressing down and out motion, until base is covered with an even layer of dough.
Bake on center rack: 6 minutes.
Pull from oven and set aside.
Pour into liquid measure then set aside: 1/3 cup raspberry sauce.
Spread remaining sauce evenly over the cooked dough.
Sprinkle rice flour, generously, over clean surface area, and coat your hands and rolling pin.
Place uncooked dough on floured surface and sprinkle dough with rice flour. Start to roll dough. Use flipper to lift dough off surface and flip over. Sprinkle surfaces with more rice flour. Roll dough until 1/4" thick. If needed use flipper to release dough from surface area. Tear pieces of the rolled dough and place over top of raspberry sauce and cooked dough.
Sprinkle with: raw almonds and 1/3 cup raspberry sauce.
Place back in oven for 20 minutes. Until top is cooked and sliced almonds taste roasted.
Let cool and serve.

Time: 1 hour

* Store in sealed container in freezer or fridge.

Lemon Almond Torte

Dairy Free - A rich, moist lemon torte with a consistency and texture like cheesecake

Serves 8

Ingredients
1 cup slivered raw almonds
3 tbsp vegetable oil or grapeseed oil
1/2 cup light brown sugar
6 large brown egg yolks and whites
1/4 tsp vanilla flavor
Approximately 3 tbsp - 4 tbsp juice of 1 medium lemon (remove seeds)
Grated zest of 1 medium lemon

Other
8" x 2" round pan
Parchment paper

Method
Blend on high in blender until powdered: almonds - or purchase powdered almonds.
Line pan with: parchment paper - leave just enough over hang to grab onto with finger tips, set aside.
Beat in a large bowl, with egg beater, on high speed until thick and pale yellow: oil, sugar and egg yolks. Place whites in a medium mixing bowl, and set aside.
Rinse eggbeaters off when finished and dry completely.

Preheat toaster oven to 325 °F (165 °C).

Stir in with wooden spoon: lightly packed powdered almonds, vanilla flavor, juice of lemon and zest of lemon.
Beat with eggbeater, in another medium or large bowl, on high speed, until white and foamy: egg whites.
Pour egg whites into almond mixture and fold in until combined.
Note: for a fluffier more soufflé like torte: Beat egg whites until soft peaks form and using a spatula scrape into batter, fold in and proceed as instructed below.
Scrape batter into the lined pan and spread evenly.
Bake in center of toaster oven for 40 minutes or until browned on top.
Remove from oven. Cool in pan for 1/2 an hour before lifting torte to counter or breadboard to cool completely. Peel parchment paper away from sides.
Serve with organic whip cream on top and/or your favorite liqueur. Dress with orange slices for a bitter bite. A light coffee, or latte complement this dish.

Time: 1hr. 40min. (includes 30 minute cooling and cleanup)

❋ **Store** in sealed container in fridge or freezer.

Mango Custard
Dairy Free

Serves 4

Ingredients
1 1/2 cups diced frozen mangoes - no sugar added
2 large brown eggs
1/2 tsp vanilla flavor
8 oz. (227g) container of imitation cream cheese (non-dairy spread)
1/4 cup white sugar - finely granulated

Method
Prepare crust (pgs.32, 33, 52, 54, 55 and 56). This is optional.
Thaw over medium heat, with lid on, for 10 minutes stirring frequently, then pour into blender and blend on high 1-1 1/2 minutes: mangoes.
Combine, in large mixing bowl, with spoon: eggs, vanilla and blended mangoes.

Preheat toaster oven to 325°F (165°C).

Add to mixing bowl: imitation cream cheese.
Tilt bowl and using a spoon, whip the imitation cream cheese against inside of bowl or use electric mixer. Whip until smooth.
Combine in: white sugar.
Pour 1/2 cup and 1 tbsp of custard mixture into each custard dish, or pour all into pie crust.
Place in oven and set timer for 35 minutes.
Cook until firm looking, but giggles in centre when moved gently.
Turn off oven, open door, pull out rack and let custard/s cool.

Time: Approximately 1 hour

* **Store** in fridge, covered.

Nutty Vanilla Lemon Meringue
Dairy Free

Makes 28

Ingredients
1/2 tsp vanilla - pure extract
1/2 tsp lemon juice
3 egg whites
1/8 tsp or less sea salt (small pinch)
1/2 cup white granulated sugar - fine
Topping
1/3 cup chopped almonds or hazel nuts

Other
Parchment paper

Method
Cut and place parchment paper over cookie sheet.
Beat with hand held electric beater on speed 3 until thick, white and foamy: vanilla, lemon juice, sea salt and egg whites.
Add slowly with beater until mixture is glossy, stands stiff and pulls away from bottom and sides of bowl: sugar.

Preheat oven to 250°F (120°C).

Form and shape meringue onto cookie sheets using spoon or icing bag. Use approximately 1/3 cup each.

Sprinkle with: nuts.
Place on rack in lower 1/3 of oven or 6" up from bottom of oven (inside measurement). It is best to bake all meringue at the same time.
Bake 34-36 minutes. Rotate rack once.
Turn off oven and let meringue coast in oven 30 minutes. Then remove.
Cool before storing.

Time: 1hr. 36 min.

* **Store** in a sealed container. Do not leave sitting out or they will go soft.

Peach Longan Custard
Serves 8 large or 12 small

Ingredients
Crust
1 large brown egg
1/4 tsp vanilla flavor
1/8 tsp sea salt
1/3 cup light brown sugar
1 1/4 cups ground, blanched, raw almonds
1 1/2 tbsp 100% grape seed oil

Filling
2 cups frozen sliced peaches - unsweetened (approximately 20 slices)
Approximately 1/3 cup of longan fruit flesh or 6 longan berries
2/3 cup granulated white sugar
5 eggs
1 2/3 cups plain cream cheese
2 tsp vanilla flavor

Other
8" x 1 1/2" round pan
Parchment paper

Method
Line 8" round by 1 1/2" deep pan with: parchment paper - press into base of pan and up the sides, trim off excess leaving just enough to grab onto, this makes it easy to pull custard out.

Preheat toaster oven to 325° F (165°C).

Prepare Crust.
Beat in large mixing bowl: egg, vanilla flavor, sea salt and sugar.
Combine in with wooden spoon: almonds and grapeseed oil.
Scrape thick and sticky mixture into the center of the pan and use the spoon to spread evenly over base until you get close as possible to inside walls of pan.
Grease fingers and spread mixture 1/2 way up sides of the pan. Poke uncooked crust all over with a fork. Place in centre of oven.
Bake 15 minutes.
Remove from oven and set aside.
Turn oven down to 300° F.
Prepare Filling.
Thaw over high heat, in a heavy sauce pan, stirring frequently: peaches.
Remove peaches from heat when completely thawed.
Peel and remove pit from: longan fruit.

Tip: Pinch top of berry shell between fingers until top of shell cracks open. Peel and remove shell, then peel flesh off of the seed.

Add to peaches: longan flesh.
Beat on medium speed for 1-2 minutes: peach and longan mixture.
Combine in: white sugar, eggs, cream cheese and vanilla flavor.

Pour into crust.
Cook 50-55 minutes. When cooked custard should giggle slightly in center, but should not be soupy. Turn off oven, open door and slide oven rack and custard out. Leave there to cool. It is important that it cools slowly.

Slice.
Serve.

Time: 1hr. 40min.

* **Store** in fridge, in sealed glass container.

Pie Crust

Dairy Free / Vegan - Makes a firm or soft light tasting crust

Makes 1 – 9" round

Ingredients

Crust
3/4 cup sorghum flour
1/2 cup brown rice flour
1/4 cup corn starch
1/8 tsp sea salt
6 tbsp grapeseed oil
3-4 tbsp organic raspberry lemonade - from concentrate

Soft Crust
For a sweeter soft crust substitute raspberry lemonade with: 1-2 tsp fine white natural granulated sugar, 1/4 tsp vanilla extract and 1-2 tbsp organic lemonade from concentrate.

Method

Preheat oven to 350°F (180°C).

Prepare filling as instructed. See Limeade Filling (pg.77) and Mango Custard (pg.49)

Note: Soft Crust is best with a light tasting filling such as lemon meringue, lime, cheese cake, pudding or custard.

Prepare Crust. Whisk in large mixing bowl: dry ingredients. Combine in with a wooden spoon, or cut in, until mixture resembles a moist crumble: wet crust ingredients. Pour into 9" glass pie plate.

Use a pressing motion with fingers to compact mixture into an even layer (approximately 3/16" - 1/4" thick) over bottom and up sides of dish. Don't leave any cracks in the shell.

Poke shell all over with fork, then place in lower 1/3 of oven (approximately 6" up from bottom of oven) for 5-7 minutes. If cooking filling longer than 20 minutes, then only pre-cook crust 2-3 minutes.

Remove from oven and let pie or shell cool before placing on cooling rack. If filling is raw or needs to be chilled in fridge, let glass cool before placing in fridge.

Slice with knife and serve with metal pie spatula.

Top with topping instructions for specific filling or for a simple fruit filling serve with whip cream or ice cream.

Tip: This pie crust is best served the following day.

Time: Approximately 25 minutes (not including filling)

* Store in fridge on pie plate, covered with plate, or follow filling instructions for storage.

Pie Crust
Dairy Free

Makes 1 - 9" round

Ingredients
2 tbsp fine white granulated sugar
1 cup brown rice flour
2 1/2 tbsp white rice flour
1/3 cup sorghum flour
2 tbsp potato flour
1/4 tsp sea salt
1/4 tsp cinnamon
1/2 tsp vanilla flavor
1/3 cup warm water
5 tbsp grapeseed oil
1 large brown egg
Fillings (pgs.49, 73, 77 and 80)

Method
Preheat oven to 350°F (180°C).

Prepare Filling.
Prepare crust while filling is cooking. Add to large mixing bowl and combine with wooden spoon until dough starts to form then collect with hands and knead in bowl several times: crust ingredients.
Grease (lightly) 9" round glass pie plate.
Place dough in 9" round glass pie plate. Use a pressing down and out motion to spread dough into an even layer (approximately 1/4" thick) over bottom and up sides of dish. Don't leave any cracks in the dough. Poke all over with fork then place in oven for 5 minutes.
Remove crust from oven and fill with: filling ingredients.
Place back in oven and cook for 15 minutes or follow instructions for specific filling times.
Remove from oven and let pie cool.
Slice and serve on plate with metal pie spatula.
Top with ice cream or whip cream (optional).

Time: 50 minutes

* **Store** pie in sealed container in fridge or freezer.

Pie Crust – White
Dairy Free

Makes 1

Ingredients
Crust
1/8 tsp sea salt
2.5 tsp fine white granulated sugar
1 cup white rice flour
1/4 cup brown rice flour
1/3 cup sorghum flour
4 tbsp grapeseed oil
2/3 cup warm water
1 large brown egg
1/2 tsp vanilla flavor
1/2 tsp cinnamon
Fillings (pgs.49, 73, 77 and 80)
Topping:
Ice cream
Whip cream

Other
1/3 cup white rice flour
9" glass pie plate
Rolling pin

Method
Preheat oven to 350°F (180°C).

Prepare Filling.
Prepare Crust. While filling is cooking add to large mixing bowl and combine with a wooden spoon until dough starts to form, then collect with hands and knead in bowl several times: crust ingredients.

Tip: best covered and refrigerated 1 hour prior to use.

Place dough in pie plate. Use a pressing down and out motion to spread dough into an even layer (approximately 1/4" thick) over bottom and up sides of dish. Don't leave any cracks in the dough. Poke all over with fork then place in oven for 5 minutes.
Remove crust from oven and fill with filling ingredients.
Roll out any excess dough and cut into strips to lay on top of filling for lattice detail. Flour clean dry counter, chopping block or wax paper; top of dough and rolling pin prior to rolling with: 1/3 cup of extra white rice flour. Use metal spatula to remove dough from surface.
Place pie back in oven and cook for 15 minutes.
Remove from oven and let pie cool.
Slice and serve on plate with metal pie spatula.
Top with ice cream, whip cream or yogurt (optional).

Time: 22 minutes for crust
65 minutes for whole pie

Pumpkin Custard
Dairy Free / Vegan

Makes 3 - 1/2 cup servings

Ingredients
Custard
1 1/3 cup cooked yam - peeled and cubed
1 cup filtered water or tap water
1 tsp freshly squeezed lemon juice
1/3 cup coconut milk solids - from top of can
3 tbsp almond milk - unsweetened/original
1 tsp vanilla - pure extract
1 cup cubed ataulfo mango
Small pinch of nutmeg
Small pinch of cinnamon
Topping
Cinnamon
Grated lemon zest
Hawaiian black lava salt or other black sea salt

Method
Wash, peel and cube yam.
Boil until yam is soft. Approximately 25 minutes. While yam is cooking, wash, peel and prepare: other ingredients.
Remove from heat and drain: water.
Remove lid to cool: yam.
Blend on high, until smooth and combined: custard ingredients.
Divide evenly into custard cups.
Chill at least 30 minutes.

Top with: cinnamon, lemon zest and sprinkle salt over top sparingly and evenly.

Time: 1 hr. 20 min.

Raw Fruit Pudding
Dairy Free / Vegan

Makes 3 - 1/2 cup servings

Ingredients
1/2 cup - 1/2 a ripe avocado cubed
1 tsp freshly squeezed lemon juice - 1/4 lemon
1 cup fresh blueberries
1 tbsp apple juice from concentrate - fancy grade
2 tbsp almond milk - unsweetened/ original
1 cup cubed mango - 1 ataulfo mango
Topping
Whip cream
Lemon zest - 1 organic lemon
Blueberries

Method
Wash, dry, and peel fruit.
Blend on high until combined and pudding consistency: Ingredients.
Top with: Topping ingredients.
Serve.

Time: 30-40 minutes

Sunflower Chocolates
Dairy Free / Vegan - A sweet bite for any event

Makes 16

Ingredients
1 cup raw hulled sunflower seeds
2 tbsp. raw sesame tahini
1 tbsp. organic sunflower seed butter or spread, or organic peanut butter
1 tbsp. organic raw blue agave nectar
.472kg block of dark couverture chocolate (l x w x d) 4 3/4" x 3 1/4" x 1 1/2"

Other
Parchment paper

Method
Blend on high in blender until mostly powdered then pour into large mixing bowl: sunflower seeds.
Stir in with wooden spoon until well combined and crumbly: sesame tahini, sunflower seed butter or spread, or organic peanut butter, and agave nectar.
Measure 1 1/2" up chocolate block and draw line. Melt down to this line over minimum heat, in small copper/stainless sauce pan, stirring frequently, or melt an entire block measuring 3 1/4" x 1 1/2" x 1 1/2".

Tip: Choose any favorite high quality chocolate to make quality tasting Sunflower Chocolates. This provides a smoother texture. For a bitter-sweet Sunflower Chocolate use unsweetened dark chocolate.
Line a large plate with: parchment paper.
Scoop sunflower seed mixture into measuring spoon, press firmly into spoon then push out of spoon into palm of hand: 1 tbsp. of sunflower seed mixture.
Squeeze firmly, rotate between fingers and palm, squeezing each rotation, or transfer mixture from palm to palm squeezing each time until balls are formed.

Tip: Rinse hand and dry off every 2nd ball. Place balls so they will not touch one another after coating with melted chocolate.

Place on parchment paper covered plate.
Remove pot from burner and pour over each sunflower ball: 1 tbsp. of chocolate.

 Note: You may need to manipulate the chocolate with the spoon (if it is thick) to cover the top and sides of the ball.

Tip: If the chocolate becomes difficult to manipulate while coating the balls put the chocolate in the small pot back on the small burner over minimum heat.

Place plate in fridge, after all balls are

coated, for about 20-30 minutes to harden chocolate.
Serve.

Time: 60 minutes

* **Store** in fridge or freezer in sealed container. Thaw in fridge or on serving plate.

Whole Egg Macaroon Base / Cookies
Dairy Free - Soft, lemony and wonderfully textured

Makes 1 - 8" x 8" square base, 3 - 3" - 3 1/2" round bases or 6 cookies

Ingredients
1 cup cold powdered almonds or almond flour
1 cold large brown egg
1 tbsp cold lemon juice - freshly squeezed
2 tbsp cold maple syrup - amber
1/8 tsp or less sea salt - 1 pinch
2 tbsp grapeseed oil
1/2 cup cold shredded coconut - sweetened

Other
Parchment paper or rice paper
Glass bakeware
Toaster oven

Method
Turn rack over in toaster oven so that it is really close to the ceramic elements.

Preheat toaster oven to 350°F (175°C).

Cut paper to desired size and place on flat bakeware. If needing to use a deep dish (without removable sides), it is best to leave a little paper overhanging to grab onto when removing dessert from bakeware.

Combine with fork in small mixing bowl: all ingredients.

Prepare cookies by scooping out and placing on paper: 6 equal portions.

Prepare base/s for cake/s or squares by placing on paper and spreading to: 8" x 8" round or square, or divide into 3 and place on paper and spread into small circles - all should be approximately 1/2" thick. If preparing an uncooked topping, bake base first and let cool.

Place in toaster oven and bake 30 minutes.
Rotate once.

Time: 40-45 minutes

* **Store** in sealed container in fridge or freezer.

Foods That Work For You: Delectable and Gluten-Free Desserts and Drinks

Drinks

Banana Lychee Smoothie...................63
Banana Shake.....................................64
Banana Vanilla Smoothie......................65
Blueberry Smoothie...........................65
Coconut Pineapple
Medley..66
Julian's Raspberry Slushy....................66
Mango Banana Smoothie.....................67

Mango Passion
Slushy...67
Mango Smoothie.............................68
Orange Tropical
Smoothie...69
Peach Smoothie..............................70
Strawberry Smoothie.......................71

Banana Lychee Smoothie

Great with a muffin or scone

Makes 2 cups

Ingredients

1 cup yogurt - 0% M.F.
1/2 a medium peeled banana - broken up
6 canned lychee - sweetened
1 cup guava and other juice fruit blend - no added sugar

Method

Combine in blender on high: all ingredients.
Blend 1 minute.
Pour into glasses.

Enjoy.

Time: 5-10 minutes

Banana Shake
Dairy free / Vegan

Makes 2 regular or 1 large

Ingredients
1 1/2 cups almond milk - unsweetened/original
1/2 tsp vanilla - pure extract
3/4 - 1 cup frozen banana (1 medium or regular size) - cut up and skin removed

Other
Blender

Method
Chop into 5 or 6 chunks, cut off skin and add to blender: frozen banana chunks.
Add to blender: milk and vanilla.
Liquefy (chop) on high for approximately 1 1/2 minutes.
Pour into glasses.
Serve right away.
Enjoy.

Tip: In the summer or in hotter climates, chill glasses in fridge or freezer.

Time: 5-7 minutes

Foods That Work For You: Delectable and Gluten-Free Desserts and Drinks

Banana Vanilla Smoothie
Dairy Free / Vegan

Makes 1 1/2 cups

Ingredients
1 1/3 cup almond milk - unsweetened/original
1 peeled small banana - broken up (approximately 3/4 cup)
1/4 tsp vanilla - pure extract

Method
Blend on high for 1 minute: all ingredients.
Pour into glasses.

Enjoy.

Time: 6-7 minutes

Blueberry Smoothie
Dairy Free / Vegan

Makes 2 cups

Ingredients
1 cup almond milk - original/unsweetened
1 cup banana - 1 medium banana peeled and broken up
1/4 cup organic coconut milk solids from top of 400ml can
1 cup frozen blueberries - unsweetened
1 cup orange - 1 medium orange peeled and sliced

Method
Prepare Ingredients.
Blend on high for 1-2 minutes or until well combined: Ingredients.

Serve.

Time: 10-12 minutes

Coconut Pineapple Medley
Dairy Free / Vegan

Makes 3 1/2 cups

Ingredients
1 cup passion fruit juice - 100% fruit juice blend - no sugar added
2 cups coconut pineapple juice - juice sweetened
1 small orange - washed, peeled and sliced
1 cup banana - 1 regular sized banana peeled and broken up

Method
Add to blender and blend on high for 1 minute, or until well combined: Ingredients.
Pour into glasses.

Time: 5-10 minutes

Julian's Raspberry Slushy
Low Fat - A refreshing, punchy slushy

Serves 4

Ingredients
1/2 cup skim milk yogurt - plain
1/2 cup 100% raspberry juice - no sugar added
1/2 cup frozen raspberries - unsweetened
1 cup frozen peaches - sliced unsweetened
1 small banana - peeled and broken up
Topping
12 whole frozen raspberries

Method
Place in blender: Ingredients.
Blend all ingredients on high until pink, smooth and thick.
Pour and divide up into: 4 glasses
Garnish each with: 3 whole frozen raspberries.

Time: 5-10 minutes

Mango Banana Smoothie
Dairy Free / Vegan

Makes 3 cups

Ingredients
1/3 cup pineapple coconut juice - juice sweetened
1 1/2 cups mango and other fruit juice blend - no sugar added
1 large banana - peeled and broken up
1 cup almond milk - original/unsweetened

Method
Add to blender: Ingredients.
Blend on high until well combined.
Pour into glasses.

Time: 6-7 minutes

Mango passion Slushy
Dairy Free / Vegan

Serves 3

Ingredients
1 cup pineapple coconut juice - juice sweetened
1 cup passion fruit juice - no sugar added
2 cups frozen diced mangoes - no sugar added

Method
Combine in blender and blend on high 1/2 - 1 minute or until all mango chunks are broken up: all ingredients.

Pour into glasses.

Time: 5-7 minutes

Mango Smoothie

Dairy Free / Vegan - Breakfast, refreshment or dessert

Makes 2 cups

Ingredients
1 1/2 cups mango juice - 100% fruit juice blend no sugar added
1 cup diced frozen mangoes - no sugar added
3/4 cup peeled banana - broken up
Topping
Fresh mango - peeled and diced or sliced
Whip cream (dairy free)

Method
Measure out and add to blender: mango juice, frozen mangoes and banana.
Blend on high for 1 minute or until well combined: Ingredients.
Peel and slice or dice a fresh mango.
Pour smoothie into glasses.
Top smoothie with: whip cream, and diced or sliced mango.

Serve.

Time: 5-10 minutes

Enjoy.

Orange Tropical Smoothie
Dairy Free / Vegan

Approximately 3 cups

Ingredients
1/2 cup fresh pineapple - diced with skin removed
3/4 cup orange - 1 small - washed, sliced and peeled
1/2 cup organic coconut milk solids from top of can
1 cup banana (1 medium ripe) - peeled and sliced
1 cup 100% orange juice
Garnish
Orange slices

Method
Blend on high for 1 minute: Ingredients.
Pour into glasses.
Garnish with: round, thin orange slice.
Cut 1/2 way into slice with knife and place over edge of glass.

Serve.

Time: 10-12 minutes

Peach Smoothie
Low Fat

Makes 2 1/2 cups

Ingredients
1/2 ripe banana - peeled and broken up
1/2 cup skim yogurt
1 cup peach juice - no sugar added
1 cup peach - 10 frozen slices

Method
Blend on low for 1/2 a minute, then on high for another 1/2 a minute or until well combined: Ingredients.
Pour into glasses.

Serve.

Time: 5-7 minutes

Strawberry Smoothie
Dairy Free / Vegan

Makes 3 cups

Ingredients
1 cup almond milk - unsweetened/original
1 small banana - peeled and broken up
1 cup whole frozen strawberries - unsweetened
1/2 cup pineapple coconut juice - juice sweetened

Method
Blend on high until well combined: Ingredients.
Pour into glasses.

Serve.

Time: 5-7 minutes

Foods That Work For You: Delectable and Gluten-Free Desserts and Drinks

Sauces and Fillings

Apple Pie Filling.....................................73
Blueberry Sauce....................................74
Cream Cheese Icing...............................75
Dark Chocolate Icing..............................76
Limeade Filling......................................77
Maple Syrup Drizzle and Peanut Taffy Topping..78
Raspberry Sauce...................................79
Strawberry Spartan Filling.....................80

Apple Pie filling
Dairy Free / Vegan

1 pies worth

Ingredients
3/4 cup filtered water
2 1/2 tbsp corn starch
1 tsp cinnamon
1/2 tsp nutmeg
8 cups - 5 sliced royal gala apples

Method
Add to large cooking pot: Ingredients.
Place over medium heat with lid on.
Stir frequently.
Prepare favorite crust (pgs.32, 33, 52, 54, 55 and 56).
Pour in filling.
Bake.

Time: 50 minutes for filling

- **Store** covered in fridge or freezer.

Blueberry Sauce

Dairy Free / Vegan - Makes a delicious quick jam, topping or filling

Approximately 2 cups

Ingredients

2 cups frozen blueberries
1/3 cup white granulated sugar

Method

Turn element on to high.
Place small, heavy sauce pan on element and add blueberries and sugar.
Place lid on pot and stir regularly.
Stir until sugar is dissolved, sauce looks soupy and it is simmering.
Turn element to medium, place lid back on.
Stir sauce regularly, for approximately 15 minutes.
Remove lid and continue to stir frequently for another 10-15 minutes and blueberries have cooked down.

Remove sauce from element.
Stir occasionally to help steam escape.

Note: sauce should be thicker and have cooked down about 1".

Serve hot, warm or cold.

Time: 15-20 minutes

- **Store** in sealed container in fridge or freezer.

- **Reheat** in sauce pan over medium to low heat and stir frequently.

Cream Cheese Icing
Dairy Free / Vegan

Tops two 8" cakes or coats 1 whole cake with left overs for individual slices

Ingredients
1 - 250g package of cream cheese 55% moisture 31% M.F. (dairy free or regular)
1/4 tsp vanilla - pure extract
2 tbsp raw blue organic agave nectar
1/8 cup freshly squeezed orange juice - 1/2 large orange, no pulp

Method
Whip until smooth: Ingredients.
Use silicone scraper and spread in an even layer over cake.

Tip: Spread over cool cake.

Time: 30 minutes or less (includes cleanup)

* **Store** in a sealed container in the fridge or freezer. Thaw in fridge.

Dark Chocolate Icing

Dairy Free / Vegan - A smooth solid icing that stays formed when cool with a matt finish

Coats outside and fills centre of 1 cake - 1 3/4" deep x 7 3/4" round

Ingredients

1/2 of 1 callebaut couverture dark chocolate block (.472kg) l x w x d (5" x 3 1/2" x 1 1/2")
1/2 cup organic coconut milk solids from top of can
7 tbsp premium cocoa

Method

Melt in small pot over minimum heat or double boiler, swirling often: 1/2 the block of chocolate (2 1/2" x 3 1/2" x 1 1/2").
Add to small mixing bowl: coconut milk solids.
Combine into warm melted chocolate: 5 tbsp cocoa.
Scrape chocolate mixture into coconut milk solids and combine in with electric beater set to power 1.
Blend in to combine - stopping once to scrape walls of mixing bowl - until thick, sticky and glossy: 2 tbsp cocoa.
Spread in an even layer (1/8" - 1/4" thick) over cake using a rubber scraper. When layering cake: cut cake in half first, spread icing, place top back on, then coat exterior.
Decorate by putting icing in pastry bag and fitting with desired nozzle.

Note: If this batter is left to sit or has been chilled, it will need to be re-blended to become spreadable.

Time: 40 minutes

- **Store** in sealed container or sealed bag in fridge or freezer.

Limeade Filling

Dairy Free - A cool summer pie with a custard / jelly consistency

Fills 1 - 9" round shell

Ingredients
1/8 tsp sea salt
2/3 - 3/4 cup fine granulated white sugar - natural
1/3 cup cornstarch
1/3 - 1/2 cup water (filtered)
1 1/2 cups organic limeade from concentrate
1 tsp organic matcha green tea powder - unsweetened
4 large egg yolks
Topping
Whip cream

Method
Prepare pie shell (pg.54) or other favorite pie shell.
Combine with whisk, in medium sauce pan: all dry ingredients.
Whisk in until combined: liquids.

Tip: You may substitute the juice with other juices like lemonade or raspberry lemonade. Just keep the liquid portions the same as the original recipe (2 cups in total) and omit matcha powder. You may add to dry ingredients: 4-5 tsp of cocoa powder - instead of matcha powder.

These two juices from concentrate tend to be sweeter than the limeade, so you may want to use the lesser amount of sugar. A meringue topping goes great with this filling. Just follow your favorite meringue topping recipe and add it to the top of the filling while it is still hot, place in the oven preheated to 325°F and bake 20 minutes.

Combine in: egg yolks.
Turn element on to medium and whisk mixture frequently. When the mixture starts to thicken, whisk continuously until steaming, bubbles form and foam has disappeared. Whisk another 5-10 minutes, remove from heat and continue whisking, approximately 2 minutes.
Pour into pie shell.
Place pie on cooling rack to cool bottom of pie before placing in fridge to cool completely - best chilled for at least 4 hours.
Serve on its own, with whip cream, or a soft meringue topping.

Time: 30-35 minutes for filling

* **Store** in fridge 3 days maximum.

Maple Syrup Drizzle and Topping
Dairy Free / Vegan

Amber Drizzle

Ingredients
Pure maple syrup - amber
Your choice of nut
Freshly squeezed lemon, orange or lime juice for citrus flavor (optional)
Salt

Method
Adjust maple syrup amount to cater to size of dish.
Adjust citrus amount to desired strength.
Add salt to taste.
Stir together with spoon: Ingredients.
Chop and add nuts, then stir in and drizzle, or sprinkle nuts over top of dish and drizzle with amber drizzle.

Time: 10-15 minutes

Peanut Taffy Topping
1 cake - 8" - 10" round

Ingredients
1/3 heaping cup of your choice nut (almonds, walnuts, pecans, or coconut)
1/8 tsp or less sea salt - 1 small pinch
1/4 tsp lemon juice - freshly squeezed
1/3 cup pure maple syrup - amber
1/4 cup brown sugar - natural/golden or demerara
1 tbsp peanut butter - natural crunchy

Method
Chop: nuts - except pre-shredded or pre-flaked coconut.
Add to mixing bowl: all ingredients - except nuts.
Combine using electric blender on low speed (2-3).
Stir in: nuts.
Drizzle or pour over tarts, muffins, pie or cheese cake 12-15 minutes before they are finished baking. Alternatively heat over medium setting (3-4), in small pot, on stove top, whisking continuously (approximately 10 minutes) or until topping just starts to thicken: all ingredients. Turn down to 1 or low, and continue whisking another 3-5 minutes.
Quickly pour over desired dessert.

Time: 24-30 minutes

Foods That Work For You: Delectable and Gluten-Free Desserts and Drinks

Raspberry Sauce
Dairy Free / Vegan - Serve over vanilla ice cream, yogurt, cakes and squares

Approximately 2 cups

Ingredients
2 cups frozen unsweetened raspberries
1/3 cup finely granulated white sugar

Method
Thaw over medium heat, in small stainless pot with lid on: raspberries.
Stir occasionally with wooden spoon until completely thawed.
Add: sugar.
Stir constantly while simmering with lid off, 5-10 minutes.
Remove from heat.
Cool berry sauce in pot.
Stir occasionally.

Time: 15-20 minutes

- **Store** in sealed container in the fridge or freezer.

- **Reheat** over medium to low heat, stirring occasionally. Do not overcook or burn (easy to do with sugary sauces).

Strawberry Spartan Filling
Dairy Free / Vegan - Taste and texture like strawberry and rhubarb

Fills 1 - 9" round shell

Ingredients
5 cups frozen whole strawberries
2 Spartan apples (approximately 2 cups) - sliced
3 1/2 tbsp corn starch - 100% pure
1 tsp cinnamon
3 tbsp fine white granulated sugar
1/4 tsp nutmeg
1/4 tsp sweet basil
1/8 tsp or less sea salt - 1 small pinch
2/3 cup water (filtered)

Method
Prepare crust (pgs.32, 33, 54, 55, and 56).
Place in a large pan over low heat with lid on: all ingredients.
Stir frequently.
Pour into crust.

Time: 40 minutes for filling

* **Store** in fridge or freezer in sealed container. Thaw in fridge.

Glossary

Foods That Work For You: Delectable and Gluten-Free Desserts and Drinks

Almond Milk or Nut Milk Made by blending almonds or other nuts, then placing them into a strainer and pouring purified or filtered water over the almond meal and letting the milk drain into a sterilized sealable glass container or jar, will keep 3 days in the refrigerator. You may use this process for making other nut or seed milks. Store bought almond milk may have additives - I use Almond Breeze for my recipes.

Calcium Powder Monocalcium phosphate is sold with methoxyl citrus pectin to produce a jelly like substance, so less sugar is needed in your jelly products. I prefer Pamona's.

Combine To thoroughly mix all ingredients together, making sure there are no lumps left and mixture is uniform.

Dice To cut food up into small squares.

Gluten A protein found in all grains. The gluten found in grains like: rye, wheat or Khorasan, and barley are not safe for people who have celiac disease or gluten intolerance.

Julienne To cut into short, thin strips.

Lychee Fruit Similar to longan fruit, only with a bumpy pointy textured skin that is a fleshy pink color. See longan fruit.

Longan Fruit Seasonal fruit found in your local food store, but mostly found in oriental stores or China town centers; may also be purchased on line. Longan fruit can be purchased fresh, canned or dried. See individual recipes for which one to use. Has a crackled, beige/green thin shell like skin covering the juicy, cooling, floral white flesh that surrounds a large brown seed.

Pectin Found in fruit. The pectin extracted from citrus peel is used in combination with monocalcium phosphate (sold together) to activate its jelling power. Used for making jams, yogurt, pie and other products needing a jelly consistency.

Separate Egg Crack egg. Separate halves. Pour yolk back and forth between shell halves over bowl, letting white fall into bowl. Place yolk in a different bowl.

Sorghum Flour A popular grain used in cereals and in baking. Can be ground into flour. For a list of GF grains see page 81.

List of Gluten-Free Grains and Casein-Free Alternatives

Important: Before trying a new product make sure to try a small amount first before purchasing a large quantity. Always look for the note "GF", "CF", "Dairy-Free" and "produced in a dedicated wheat-free, gluten-free facility" on packaging or equivalent. When in doubt, call the number and ask before purchasing. The same goes for dairy-free products.

GF - Flour / Whole / Ground / Powdered / Starch

- Amaranth
- Arrowroot
- Beans
- Buckwheat
- Corn (Maize)
- Flax
- Garfava
- Millet
- Nut Flours
- Potato
- Quinoa
- Rice
- Seed Flours
- Sorghum
- Soy
- Tapioca
- Teff

CF

- Butters - Seeds and Nuts
- Dairy-Free - Yogurts, Soups, Milks and Desserts
- Italian Ices
- Kosher Foods
- Milks - Bean, Seed, Nut, or Potato
- Soy - Cheeses, Milks, Tofu and Ice Creams

Links to Dairy-Free / Gluten-Free / Soy-Free / Nut- Free / Non GMO and Vegan Chocolate Options - Bars, Cocoa, Chips and more:

www.ahlaska.com/about_us.aspx
www.bbfdirect.com/pc/pascha-chocolate
http://cocorawchocolate.com/collections/solo-bars
http://www.enjoylifefoods.com/chocolate-for-baking/
www.ghirardelli.com
http://www.tastethedream.com/products/category/493.php
http://www.vivani-chocolate.de/P_Sortiment_e.html

Index
Foods That Work For You: Delectable and Gluten-Free Desserts and Drinks

Page numbers in *italics* refers to images.

A
Almond
    Cookies 8, *8*
    Cookies, Coconut 18
    Torte, Lemon *47*, 48
Amaranth 5
Amber Corn 30, *31*
Amber Drizzle 78
Apple
    Pie Filling 73
    Strawberry Spartan Filling *29*, 80
    Tarts 32

B
Banana
    Bread 9
    Coconut Cream Pie 33
    Custard 35, *35*
    Lychee Smoothie 63
    Pecan Muffins *10*, 11
    Shake 64
    Smoothie, Mango 67, *67*
    Vanilla Smoothie 65
Bars
    Coffee Toffee *42*, 43
Berries
    Blackberry Scones *12*, 13
    Blueberry Pretzel Tarts, Maple 24, *25*
    Blueberry Sauce 74, *74*
    Blueberry Smoothie 65, *65*
    Julian's Raspberry Slushy 66
    Layered Raspberry Squares 46
    Raspberry Sauce 79, *79*
    Raw Fruit Pudding 58, *58*
    Strawberry Smoothie 71
    Strawberry Spartan Filling *29*, 80
Biscuits, Pretzel *25*, 26
Blackberry Scones *12*, 13
Blueberry Pretzel Tarts, Maple 24, *25*
Blueberry Sauce 74, *74*
Blueberry Smoothie 65, *65*
Boule De Neige À La Mousse 36, *37*
Bread
    Banana 9
    Goodies 7, *7*
Brownie Cake 38, *39*
Buckwheat
    Chocolate Chip Cookies 14
    Shortbread 15, *15*

C
Cakes
    Brownie 38, *39*
    Corn 19, *72*
    Dark Chocolate 45
Cheese Icing, Cream 75
Chocolate
    Boule De Neige À La Mousse 36, *37*
    Brownie Cake 38, *39*
    Cake, Dark 45
    Chip Cookies, Buckwheat 14
    Cocoa Rice Puff Refrigerator Cookies 40
    Cocoa Torte 41
    Coffee Toffee Bars *42*, 43
    Icing, Dark 76
    Pecan Cookies 16, 17
    Seed Muffins, Dark *20*, 21
    Sunflower Chocolates 59, *60*
Cocoa Rice Puff Refrigerator Cookies 40
Cocoa Torte 41
Coconut
    Almond Cookies 18
    Cream Pie, Banana 33
    Pineapple Medley 66
    Whole Egg Macaroon

Base/Cookies 61
Coffee Toffee Bars 42, 43
Cookies
    Almond 8, 8
    Buckwheat
      Chocolate Chip 14
    Buckwheat
      Shortbread 15, 15
    Chocolate Pecan 16, 17
    Cocoa Rice Puff
      Refrigerator 40
    Coconut Almond 18
    Ginger Molasses 22, 23
    Snowball Shortbread 27, 28
    Whole Egg
      Macaroon Base/
        Cookies 61
Corn
    Amber 30, 31
    Cake 19, 72
    -meal Muffins 19
Cream Cheese Icing 75
Crumble
    Peanut Taffy
      Topping Crumble 11
Crusts
    Apple Tarts 32
    Banana Coconut
      Cream Pie 33
    Peach Longan
      Custard 52, 53
    Pie 54
    Pie 55, 55
    - White, Pie 56

Custards
    Banana 35, 35
    Mango 49
    Peach Longan 52, 53
    Pumpkin 57, 57
D
Dairy Free
    8, 9, 11, 13, 16, 19, 21, 23, 24, 26, 32, 33, 35, 40, 41, 48, 49, 50, 54, 55, 56, 57, 58, 59, 61, 64, 65, 66, 67, 68, 69, 71, 73, 74, 75, 76, 77, 78, 79, 80
Dark Chocolate Cake 45
Dark Chocolate Icing 76
Dark Chocolate Seed
    Muffins 20, 21
Desserts 29, 29
Drinks 62, 62
Drizzle, Amber 78
E
Eggs
    Limeade Filling 77
    Mango Custard 49
    Nutty Vanilla Lemon
      Meringue 50, 51
    Peach Longan
      Custard 52, 53
    Whole Egg
      Macaroon
        Base/Cookies 61
F
Fillings, Sauces and 72, 72
    Apple Pie 73
    Banana Coconut
      Cream Pie 33
    Limeade Filling 77

Strawberry Spartan 29, 80
Flax 5
Fruit
    Raw Fruit Pudding 58, 58
G
Ginger Molasses Cookies 22, 23
Gluten free grains 4, 5
Goodies, Bread 7, 7
Grains
    Amaranth 5
    Buckwheat 5
    Corn 4
    Flax 5
    Hemp 5
    Millet 4
    Quinoa 5
    Rice 4, 5
    Sorghum 5
H
Hemp 5
I
Icing
    Cream Cheese 75
    Dark Chocolate 76
J
Julian's Raspberry Slushy 66
L
Layered Raspberry Squares 46
Lemon Almond Torte 47, 48
Lemon Meringue, Nutty
    Vanilla 50, 51
Limeade Filling 77
Longan Custard, Peach 52, 53

Lychee Smoothie, Banana   63

M

Macaroon Base/Cookies, Whole Egg   61
Mango Banana Smoothie   67, *67*
Mango Custard   49
Mango Passion Slushy   67, *67*
Mango Smoothie   68
Maple Blueberry Pretzel Tarts   24, *25*
Maple Syrup Drizzle and Topping   78
Matcha
    Limeade Filling   77
Medley, Coconut Pineapple   66
Meringue, Nutty Vanilla Lemon   50, *51*
Millet   *4*
Molasses
    Cookies, Ginger   *22*, 23
Mousse, Boule De Neige À La   36, *37*
Muffins
    Banana Pecan   *10*, 11
    Cornmeal   19
    Dark Chocolate Seed   *20*, 21

N

Notes   6
Nuts
    Almond
        8, 18, 30, 46, 50
    Almond Flour
        8, 18, 23, 36, 41, 43, 46, 48, 52, 61
    Almond Milk
        9, 13, 16, 19, 35, 57, 58, 63, 64, 65, 67, 71
    Coconut
        18, 40, 43, 61, 78
    Coconut Milk
        33, 35, 36, 40, 45, 57, 64, 65, 68, 69, 76
    Hazel Nut
        50, 76
    Peanut Butter
        59, 78
    Pecan
        9, 11, 16, 30, 78
    Walnut
        11, 30, 78
Nutty Vanilla Lemon Meringue   50, *51*

O

Orange Tropical Smoothie   69, *69*

P

Passion Slushy, Mango   67, *67*
Peach Longan Custard   52, 53
Peach Smoothie   70, *70*
Peanut Taffy Topping   78
Pecan Cookies, Chocolate   16, *17*
Pecan Muffins, Banana   *10*, 11
Pies
    Apple   73
    Banana Coconut Cream   33
    Limeade   77
    Strawberry Spartan   *29*, 80
Pie Fillings
    Apple   73
    Banana Coconut Cream   33
    Limeade   77
    Strawberry Spartan   *29*, 80
Pineapple Medley, Coconut   66
Pretzel Biscuits   *25*, 26
Pretzel Tarts, Maple Blueberry   24, *25*
Puddings
    Raw Fruit   58, *58*
Pumpkin Custard   57, *57*

Q

Quinoa   5

R

Raspberry
    Sauce   79, *79*
    Slushy, Julian's   66
    Squares, Layered   46
Raw Fruit Pudding   58, *58*
Rice
    Puff Refrigerator Cookies, Cocoa   40

S

Sauces and Fillings   72, *72*
    Blueberry   74, *74*
    Raspberry   79, *79*
Scones
    Blackberry   *12*, 13
Seeds

Cocoa Rice Puff Refrigerator Cookies 40
Dark Chocolate Seed Muffins *20, 21*
Sunflower Chocolates 59, *60*

Shake
    Banana 64

Shortbreads
    Buckwheat 15, *15*
    Snowball 27, *28*

Slushies
    Julian's Raspberry 66
    Mango Passion 67, *67*

Smoothies
    Banana Lychee 63
    Banana Vanilla 65
    Blueberry 65, *65*
    Coconut Pineapple Medley 66
    Mango 68
    Mango Banana 67, *67*
    Orange Tropical 69, *69*
    Peach 70, *70*
    Strawberry 71

Snowball Shortbread 27, *28*
Sorghum 5
Spartan Filling, Strawberry *29*, 80
Squares
    Layered Raspberry 46
Strawberry Smoothie 71
Strawberry Spartan Filling *29*, 80
Sunflower Chocolates 59, 60
Syrup Drizzle and Topping, Maple 78

T
Taffy Topping, Peanut 78
Tarts
    Apple 32
    Maple Blueberry Pretzel 24, *25*
Toffee
    Bars, Coffee *42, 43*
Topping, Peanut Taffy 78
Torte
    Cocoa 41
    Lemon Almond *47, 48*
Tropical Smoothie, Orange 69, *69*

V
Vanilla Lemon Meringue, Nutty 50, *51*
Vanilla Smoothie, Banana 65
Vegan
    35, 40, 54, 57, 58, 59, 64, 65, 66, 67, 68, 69, 71, 73, 74, 75, 76, 78, 79, 80

W
- White, Pie Crust 56
Whole Egg Macaroon Base/Cookies 61

Y
Yam
    Pumpkin Custard 57, *57*

Gluten-Free Bakeries and Cafés

Below are some bakeries and cafés in Canada offering gluten-free menus and baked goods:

Aidan's
http://aidansglutenfree.com/index.html
Ontario

Cackling Goose Market GF Bakery Café
http://cacklinggoosemarket.ca/
38 York St, Sackville, NB

Chocolate Claim
http://chocolateclaim.com/
305 Strickland Street, Whitehorse, YT Y1A 2J9

Cookie Stéfanie
http://www.cookiestefanie.com/
272 St Jacques Ouest, Montreal, QC H2Y 1N3

Crave Cookies and Cupcakes
http://www.cravecupcakes.ca/menu/gluten-free.html
318 Aspen Glen Landing SW, Unit 106, Calgary, AB T3H 0N5

Gleneagle Gourmet Bakery
978 Cole harbour Rd, Dartmouth, NS B2V 1E7

GF Patisserie
http://www.gfpatisserie.com/

Kinnikinnick Foods Inc.
http://consumer.kinnikinnick.com/index.cfm/fuseaction/consumer.home.html
10940-120 St Edmonton, Alberta Canada T5H 3P7

Kneaded Bake shop
http://kneadedbakeshop.com/
#100 - 3725 Pasqua St., Regina, Saskatchewan, Canada

Laughing Daughters' Bakery
http://www.theceliacscene.com/240-gluten-free-Shopping-Laughing-Daughters-Bakery.html

Lemonade Gluten Free Bakery
http://www.lemonadebakery.ca/
3385 Cambie St. Vancouver, B.C. V5Z 2W6

Nourish - A Gluten-Free Bakery
http://www.nourishnewfoundland.ca/collection#!__collection
1304 Topsail Road in Paradise, NL.

Origin Bakery
http://originbakery.com/
1525 Pandora Ave. Victoria, B.C. Canada
1790 Island Highway #110 Victoria, B.C. Canada V9B 1H5

Santé - Gluten-Free Café
http://www.santeglutenfreecafe.com/
2630-A Quadra Street, Victoria BC V8T 4E4

Sophia's Bakery and Café
http://sophiasbakery.ca/
60 Colborne Street Corner of King St. & Colborne St. Brantford ON

The Gluten Free Epicurean
http://www.glutenfreeepicurean.ca/home.htm
633 East 15th Ave. Vancouver, B.C. V5T 2R6

www.ingramcontent.com/pod-product-compliance
Lightning Source LLC
Chambersburg PA
CBHW041515220426
43668CB00002B/32